EXCLAMATION POINTS SAY "WOW!"

written by MICHAEL DAHL

illustrated by CHRIS GARBUTT

PICTURE WINDOW BOOKS
a capstone imprint

Wow! This is great!
I have a whole page to myself!
This is amazing! Hey out there!
Great to meet you! I'm an
exclamation point!

We are all exclamation points!
We all have a dot and a vertical line!
Vertical means straight up and down.
You always find us at the end of a word or a sentence!
Now I DON'T have the page all to myself!

Exclamation points
are easy to find.

Exclaim means to write or say something with lots of energy!

Exclamation points show lots of excitement.

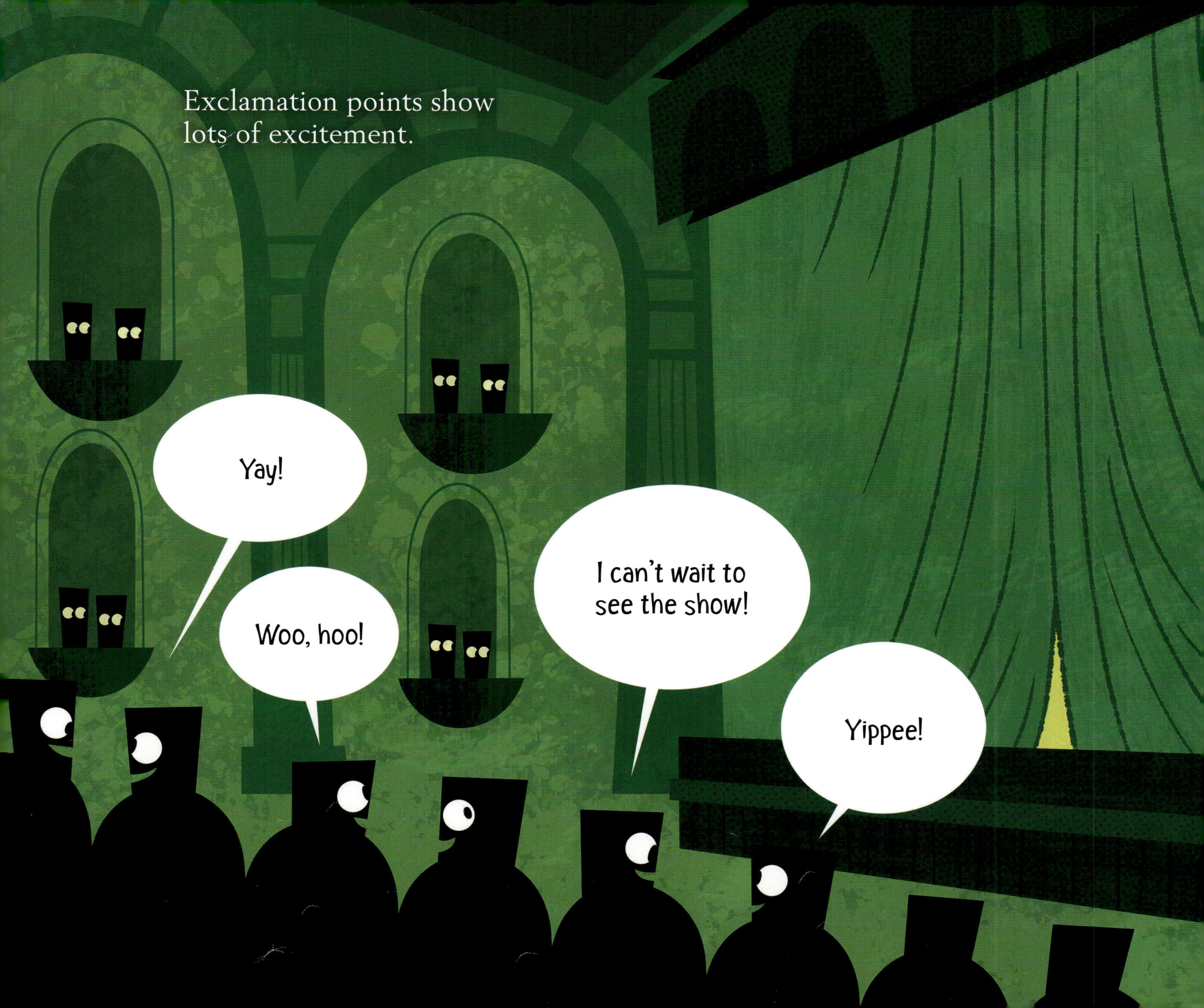

Exclamation points
also show surprise.

Look! It's just us!
Ha!

Exclamation points
can show anger.

Exclamation points can show approval.

Exclamation points are very good at telling someone they have done well.

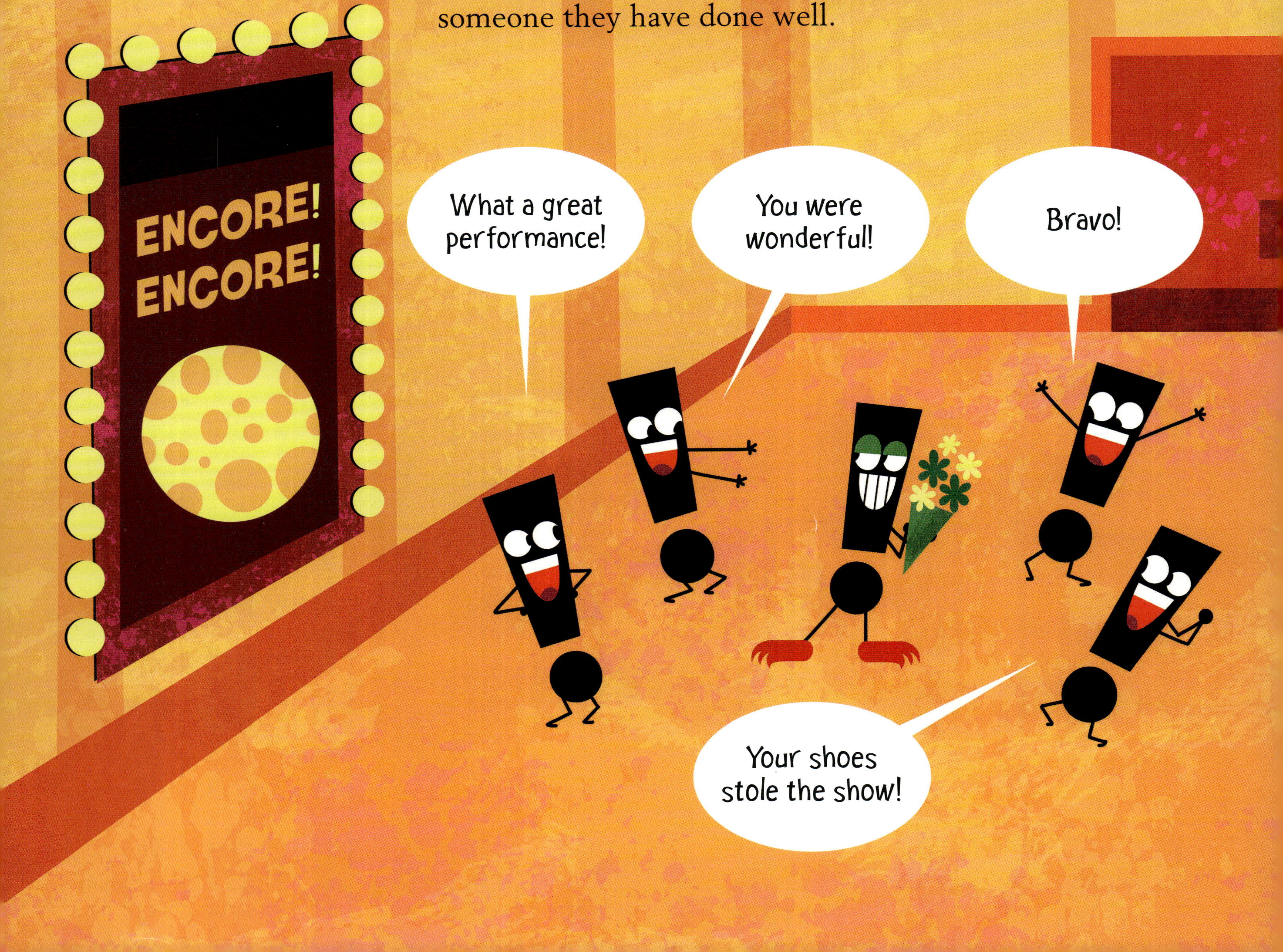

Exclamation points are good at giving commands.

Exclamation points help you agree with something.

Exclamation points also help you disagree or point out mistakes.

Exclamation points sometimes
give you warnings.

Hurry up!
STOP!
Slow down!
Careful!
Look out!

They can also give you bad news.

How awful!
Shocking!
We are off to the hospital!

Exclamation points are a part of sound effects.

TINKLE!
TINKLE!
TINKLE!
CLOMP!
CLOMP!
SQUEAK!
SQUEAK!

Even though exclamation points are fun to use, don't use too many.

HIP, HIP, HOORAY!!!!
I have more exclamation points if you need them!
!

But most important of all,
exclamation points say . . .

And thanks for closing the book! I need some rest!
Thanks! Thanks a lot!
You look shockingly exhausted!

SPOTLIGHT ON

An exclamation point is found at the end of a sentence. It shows ENERGY or EXCITEMENT.

Sometimes an exclamation point can show SURPRISE.

Other times an exclamation point can express ANGER or GIVE BAD NEWS.

EXCLAMATION POINTS

An exclamation point can also show APPROVAL or AGREEMENT.

An exclamation point is good at giving COMMANDS or WARNINGS.

An exclamation point is LOUD!
It often follows a SOUND EFFECT.

ABOUT THE AUTHOR

Michael Dahl is the author of more than 200 books for children and has won the AEP Distinguished Achievement Award three times for his nonfiction. He is the author of the bestselling *Bedtime for Batman* and *You're A Star, Wonder Woman!* picture books. He has written dozens of books of jokes, riddles, and puns. He likes to play with words. In grade school, he read the dictionary for fun. Really. And his favorite words are adverbs (*really* is an adverb, by the way).

ABOUT THE ILLUSTRATOR

Chris Garbutt hails from a family of tea-drinking hedgehogs that live deep in the magical hills of Yorkshire in the north of England. He has spent most of his time on this planet drawing cartoons and comics in London, Paris, and most recently Los Angeles, where he now creates funny pictures in exchange for cake. Most recently he has been the executive producer, show-runner, and art director of a new TV series he co-created at Nickelodeon called *Pinky Malinky*, which will be available on Netflix in 2019.

GLOSSARY

approval—the acceptance of something

command—a statement that tells someone to do something

excitement—showing lots of happy energy

exhausted—very tired or sleepy

sound effect—a written word that shows a sound made by an animal or machine; it is not always a real word

vertical—straight up and down

warning—telling someone to be careful

READ MORE

Cleary, Brian P. *The Punctuation Station*. Minneapolis: Millbrook Press, 2010.

Dahl, Michael. *Periods Say, "Stop."* Mankato, MN: Capstone Press, 2019.

Hopkins, Lee Bennett. *A Bunch of Punctuation: Poems*. Honesdale, Pa.: Wordsong, 2018.

CRITICAL THINKING QUESTIONS

1. What kind of sentence gives a command? Give an example.

2. Exclamation points tell us when a sentence is about something exciting. What makes you excited? Can you think of three things that excite you?

INTERNET SITES

Use FactHound to find Internet sites related to this book.

Visit *www.facthound.com*

Just type in this code: 9781515838630 and go.

OTHER TITLES IN THE SERIES

Commas Say "Take a Break"
Periods Say "STOP."
Question Marks Say "What?"

Editor: Shelly Lyons
Designer: Aruna Rangarajan and Hilary Wacholz
Creative Director: Nathan Gassman
Production Specialist: Tori Abraham
The illustrations in this book were created digitally.

Picture Window Books
are published by Capstone,
1710 Roe Crest Drive,
North Mankato, Minnesota 56003
www.mycapstone.com

Library of Congress Cataloging-in-Publication Data is available on the Library of Congress website.
ISBN 978-1-5158-3863-0 (library binding)
ISBN 978-1-5158-4057-2 (paperback)
ISBN 978-1-5158-3867-8 (eBook PDF)

Summary: Exclamation points make noise! They shout and command. Follow along and learn all about the importance of exclamaiton points.

Printed and bound in the USA.
PA49